A Summarized Pragmatic Study of Political
Efficiency of Social Control

Achronia and Social Control

DR.SC. GERGANA PENCHEVA-APOSTOLOVA

authorHOUSE®

AuthorHouse™ UK
1663 Liberty Drive
Bloomington, IN 47403 USA
www.authorhouse.co.uk
Phone: 0800 047 8203 (Domestic TFN)
*   +44 1908 723714 (International)*

Published by AuthorHouse 09/13/2019

ISBN: 978-1-7283-9349-0 (sc)
ISBN: 978-1-7283-9348-3 (e)

Print information available on the last page.

Any people depicted in stock imagery provided by Getty Images are models, and such images are being used for illustrative purposes only. Certain stock imagery © Getty Images.

This book is printed on acid-free paper.

Contents

OFF TIME

The White king
From the chessboard reality of Alice
Is murmuring
Tasting the sounding:
Important - unimportant
Next trying changing their places Unimportant - important finding
      no difference.
I have lost their spaces either
In the meantime of timelessness
When things fade down to shadows
Projected as images only
No heroes nor giants,
Not even dwarfs,
Just gnomes
Keeping pots of gold
Deep under the caves of history
In unreal illusions and dreams
Of microscopic
Particles
Taking place in the creation of Stars.

PREFACE

The Achronia project is focused on a set of mechanisms for social control whose reconstructions can prove applicable as a remedial and prevention complex technique in cases of unrest and upsurge of civic anxiety in times of historic crises. It is rooted in the idea for government and binding where 'social binders' are seen as sets of positive and negative tools for public mind control. A Machiavellian in nature, this study is placed in the context of Vernadski's idea of the noosphere. It is where philosophy goes ahead of knowledge and makes prevention of catastrophe possible by spreading the peaks of anxiety sending away the doers, the makers, the thinkers i.e. all the creative and productive individuals who try to resist social chaos by logical and ethic models of leadership. The modelling of the mechanism has two directions: leading and survival.

Aspects of achronia have been known and applied ever since the dawn of human culture. The mechanism has not been purposefully approached, though, and there are no descriptions of it as such, whatsoever. I have chosen to give it the name 'achronia' since it acts as a time machine where the current awareness of social affairs is beyond the time-frontiers of events where it is possible to influence them.

The description of achronia follows a number of steps:

1) Planning of social reaction through time in terms of regulation of migration; dislocation and concentration of communities; a Smithsonian approach to current division of labor.

2) Typology of achronia.

3) Varying stages of the awareness of the application of achronia by the governing bodies.

4) Achronia in modelling e-government.

5) A very recent development: tracing the dynamic features of achronia in literary texts that establish the ethos of a current culture and support public discourse. A simple model of off-time migration is achieved, allowing its redirection by means of forming e-culture where reality-weaving comes up as the basic mechanism of mindwork.

Keywords
Achronia, social binders, migration of productive generations, injustice, absurdity.

The sufferance of our souls, the time's abuse

Julius Caesar, Act 2 Scene 1

Introduction

In the following text I shall outline the description of an existing complex method of social control with long-lasting and exponentially growing, in both its depth and spread, effect, directing the expansion and survival of humanity in its changing cultural dimensions. It is immanent for the socio-historic display of existence as a strategy of humanity manifested at different level of awareness on the part of the empowered as well as under diverse guise of opposition to the applied mechanisms of social control.

The peaks of historic manifestations of this complex' effects tend to show up in times of historic crises and affect the physical boundaries of human existence. Its basis is disproportion of social layers and it is followed by surges of migration.

The perceivable part of this socio-historic complex is in the vast number of cases or individual stories held in historical records, where injustice is the challenge for common reason. Their study is an enchanting and engulfing procedure with numerous false paths and dead ends due to the intransparency of political action applied by the rulers at diverse stage of awareness or intuitive activities and followed, avoided or opposed by survivors individually.

Here I shall outline its clear types and the tangible connections to e-government where human survival has acquired virtual dimension.

The methodology of this study is based on a systematic integrated approach to the Net (SIAN) and the virtual dimension of humanity I have called 'E-kind'. It is diachronic and mentalist.

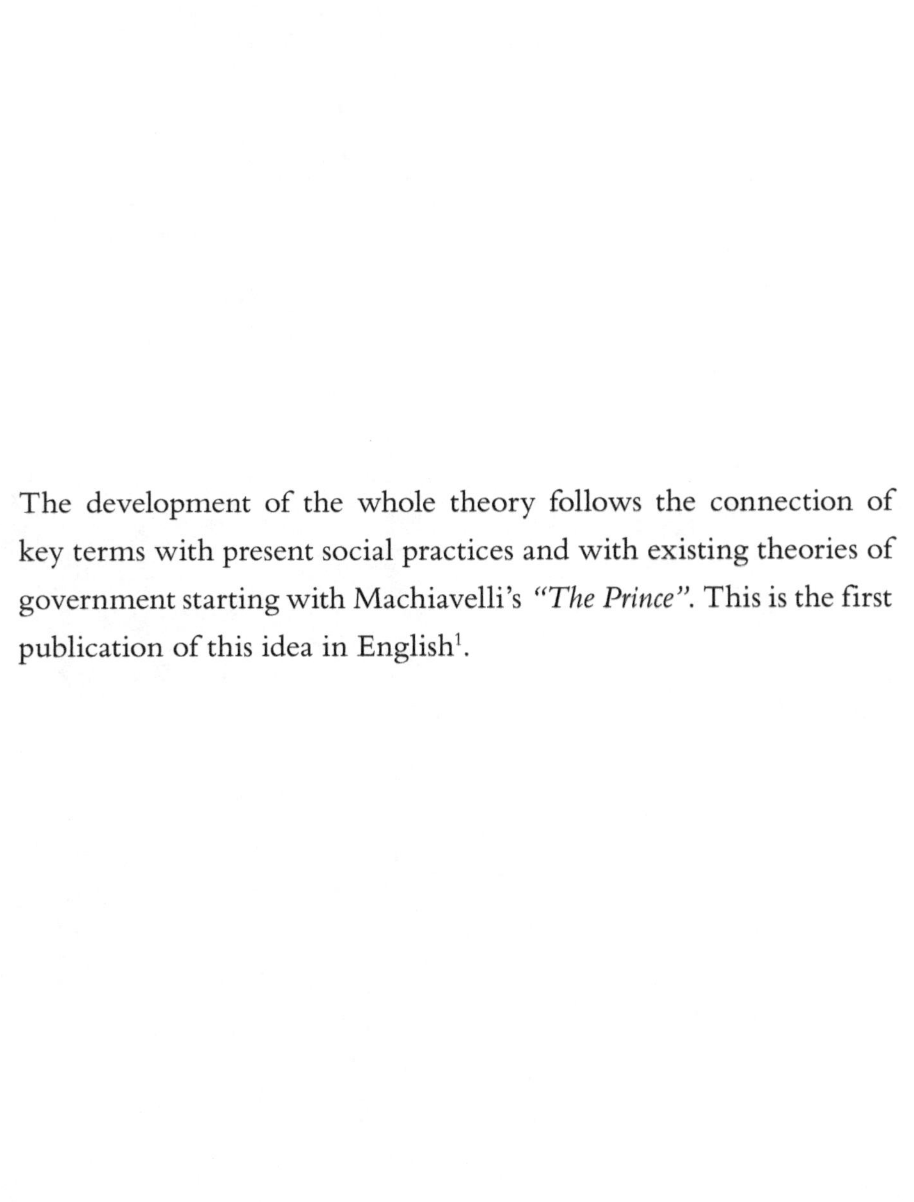

The development of the whole theory follows the connection of key terms with present social practices and with existing theories of government starting with Machiavelli's *"The Prince"*. This is the first publication of this idea in English[1].

MOTIVATION OF SEARCH

There was no name to unite the host of cases that made me search for their common features and occurrences in history, and concerning both subjects of power: the governing and the governed.

Starting from my Bulgarian books of the Iron Wall period of control I reached to Machiavelli's translation into Bulgarian finding the starting driving force for the mentalist and philosophical approached to my yet unclear subject of interest for the concept of it had no name. It was 'injustice' in its strongest and clearest sounding as shared by groups of people that formed new cultures in times of social unrest and migration, followed by mind-devastating upsurge of nostalgia.

> Whence things have their origin, thence also their destruction happens, according to necessity; for they give to each other justice and recompense for their injustice in conformity with the ordinance of Time.
>
> Anaximander, 6th C. AD Curd, Patricia, A Pre-Socratic Reader: Selected Fragments and Testimonia (Hackett Publishing, 1996), p. 12.

Into that from which things take their rise they pass away once more, as is ordained; for they make reparation and satisfaction to one another for the injustice according to the appointed time.

(Lord) Russell, A history of western philosophy Simon and Schuster, 1945 (reprint) ISBN 0-671-20158-1 Retrieved 2014-03-10

The Idea suddenly rose up with the pressing awareness of injustice at a moment when a couple of repeating cases suddenly connected in a general technique for searching a way out of the dead time before the culmination of crisis, when there was no way out to be seen:

First came the appeal of the minister of culture to the assembled agora of the World philosophy congress in Athens in the summer of 2016 summer: he directly asked for help in thinking suggestions out of the Greek crisis. The Greek colleagues immediately started whistling and protesting loudly while the rest of the philosophers wondered at their reaction. It was an embarrassing situation for the Greek thinkers that humiliated them as incapable of their work in front of some two thousand philosophers from all over the world.

Next I was invited to a department meeting in the quality of a reviewer in a professor's procedure. There was a parallel procedure for an associate professor where the candidate had used a fraud concerning her scientific production and contributions. The assembly did not vote for either procedure, leaving the decision to higher councils and, mainly, to time. Thus the really productive colleague of international significance was suppressed and sacrificed for the general fear and incapacity of the council to cope with an academic criminal case that would have ruined the department publicly.

The third case was at my own university where the department which had the highest enrollment of first year undergraduates was severely tracized while those who could not do anything for the university were saved and given the responsibility to plan and direct the next activities of the faculty. It was at that moment when the simple manipulative technique of the dean became clear: he was intuitively doing the right thing while thinking of his revenge for past disobedience and being completely unaware of what act in favor of the future he was completing.

The three cases suddenly connected with a host of cases the Bulgarian society has undergone in the past over quarter of a century to display the ethical model of the crisis of stagnation before catastrophe: the layers of self-esteem of the subjects of the situation were diametrically opposed to the historic or objective truth and thus placed the subjects of the planned action (the productive forces of a new model) out of time.

All cases were accompanied by strong reaction that modelled the aspect of pathos in the situations of analogous character: a marked display of the feeling for injustice reaching to the self-esteem of 'a lost generation' and an action of practical self-establishment to the contrary position of not being a loser. In all cases the subjects of the targeted action of rule lose their position in the current time bound social development model and become 'exiles in time' or outsiders to their culture[2]

Getting back to the three starter-cases, we can also note that academic productive elite was the target: people who work with information, who can search for and find out information, who can connect information of varying nature and produce new information in our age of information, that could serve the governing body as the fundament for a turn in their governing strategy and a solution out of the crisis.

The visible social change was expressed by movement of great groups of productive individuals in search of their new cultural and social placement: migration and its milder and mediated by government form of mobility.

The rhetoric of the social practices of the yet unformed concept of mechanism for control proved mighty and prolific, since it is based on the triadic rhetoric criteria of ethos, pathos and logos and contains all verbal guises of rule and its rejection: logos, fate, law, determination, dictum, oppression, rebuttal, freedom etc. continuing with set phrases, narrative and declaration, to reach the grounds of metaphor and beyond it where demetaphorized structure becomes a denotate of social occurrence. The rhetoric of the studied complex forms a separate project of investigation. Its study is significant to the isolation of the features that belong to our object of study from the other aspects of social control that are mixed with it in history and obscure it.

Looking at the grounds of the rising feeling of injustice we meet the frontiers of existence in the belief that 'all men are born equal': another unclear concept, applied as the illusory abstraction of *'The Promised Land'*.

I shall not go further in the enchanting wealth of data for my further case study in this paper, but return to the main line of reasoning that has motivated it.

The name of this complex product of social control thus came from the displacement of the reacting targeted subjects of social action mentally against their historically formed self-esteem: a diachronic displacement of ethos, that breaks the unity of time, place and action in each individual's story or in each individual ethic paradigm having the significance of subjective contribution to history, and finally reaching to the effect of time machine that has removed the value of history from the mentality of the productive forces of a future action.

The targeted subjects thus can be seen as the carriers of different ethos that places them in the role of generators of new cultures viewing generations still inexistent, out of time seen as the flow of current history. The study in detail of the cases of the described type hypothetically is to reach the model of controlling activities in current social processes, as well as the reconstruction of the effects of past planned control, finally to give a fundament for future prognoses of possible action and its possible effects and planned changes in their humane perspective. The whole complex acts as a time machine that can move chronotopes and create pressure on individual participation in history. It is based on social memory and is the mental mechanism that stops inertia and saves existence. Therefore, I chose the name of 'achronia'[3].

Although it is known to humanity, achronia has not been described as a complex mechanism for social control in serious texts for it is very close to what has been accepted as the natural flow of history and is disguised by its rhetoric veils and its psychological nature which has not been in the focus of past theories of power but for the rules to be followed by a 'Prince' (which also prevented them from the weaknesses of the human brain affected by prick of conscience and kept awake). The aspects of achronia, though, have been thoroughly studied and described secretly or openly, and served governors and their economic and ideological systems for political control.[4] Probably, that is due to the incomplete awareness of governors of their own activities which followed step by step with the accumulation of governing experience and the uneven opening of the information for public access. The opening of information technologically, needs however, a new stage of keeping the secrets of good governance where communities of individuals are involved to their awareness and acceptance of social injustice to good common reasoning.

Achronia has been recorded as examples, stories and sets of rules in history[5], ethical theories[6], the myths and the epic stories of humankind[7], oratory and political declarations, and in the 20th century in the theories of PR[8], media and communication, dystopia and fantasy of psychohistory[9], and, specifically in the applied field of the specific psycho-social theory of social anxiety and control[10].

In philosophy and theology 'injustice' is one of the oldest ethical terms[11] while in Machiavellian theory it is connected with the reasonably accepted idea of power exercised in a state of awareness[12].

History has saved two basic modes of migration: ecological or naturally-bound and bee swarm type based on political, professional, cultural, etc. community overload. In both cases the more productive and stable individuals migrate. They usually do not comply with tradition and become outsiders by force of their natural inclination to look for a better life for themselves and their nearest family, clan, community, society members thus turning into leaders of a higher level or members of social groups of a higher level of self-esteem who throw away guilt and anxiety as binders to tradition and fear that is based on the reduced value of the loss. They set free of historic binders and take on the risk of producing or joining a new stage of culture.

The features of the complex of achronia do not place it out of history altogether: achronia follows its stages of enacting, exit of general flow of social life, growth of creativity and steading back to time. It has always been global because it serves as a mechanism for synchronizing the creative power of humanity through displacement of the focus of division of labor in a global plan: geographically and in growth of structures of higher levels.

The markers of inactivated achronia are the turning upside down of the social scale of values, the refusal of taking on guilt, paranoiac treatment of the hidden and false aspects of official history; nostalgia for the lost kingdom (civilization, native people, birthplace, country, history, self-identity, nature, etc.); strong feeling for social injustice; lost leadership; shift of social blame onto science and education[13], Luddite behavior, tidal migration to the West, existential fear. The spaces of achronia enlarge with each next outburst.

The instruments of the achronia complex have antinomic character and are grouped to form antinomic structures of act – counteract where the two ends are not synchronized purposefully but meet to the same effect.

Obstacles to achieving the model of achronia: We are all submerged in our historic beliefs and conventions and consequently we are charged with the feeling of our own responsibility or blame for the current state of affairs. This prevents us to form judgment based on reason under the pressure of current moments. Achronia is based in the social mind of humanity and it functions in our mental projections of our selves independent of our awareness of it while its two ends of action and rejection are in the state of active opposition. The individual mind is unable to bring about all vast changes in the historical twists and turns of power, and it is also incapable of judging the current stage of social control. The pressing role of individual survival obscures the tangible sides of control. Another abstacle is the spreading mass information. Publicity needs information and the mechanisms of control need sophistication of their public image.

The opening information to broad public is the most important part of the starting mechanism of achronia. The load of information in the mental space of its keepers inevitably reaches a stage of producing leaks and creating opposition to control. Achronia does not create prevention mechanisms that can reduce it but gets larger at each next stage.

Today virtual space supports the flourishing of achronia and extends the mental projections of existence. The oppositions within the complex of achronia achieve virtual dimensions and lead to the hypothesis of its broadened scope as a mechanism for social control.

TOWARDS A GENERAL MODEL OF ACHRONIA

Technically the general idea of achronia is based on the government and binding theory[14]. Social binders are seen as fixed sets of positive and negative instruments for planned changes in social mind. The effect is directed at the level of ethos and its target is the current value system of a culture: the crash of ideal serves as the displacement mechanism of the ideas of good and bad. That affects the rhythm of the emotional aspects of individual self-esteem and henceforth to the individual's self-identity and will for belonging to the current culture. Politically the formation of fluctuating communities of unstable longevity arises as a reaction to the historic frame and serves as a mechanism for the removal of history from the individual mind. I state this on the grounds of the still unfinished displacement of the social minds of East European cultures undergoing their crises of rebuttal, and in particular, the achronia ruling in Bulgaria.

If we approach achronia from the triadic entity of ethos, pathos and logos as criteria of publicity, there are a couple of antinomies to trace: knowledge and beliefs; logic and poetics; thinking and speaking; I and the others; just and unjust; normal and absurd. The concept of power or control, however, has remained at the previous level of outburst of achronia.

The logos of achronia is based on recurrent success of governors in history and the control over the creative individuals who are pressed to invent the next vehicle of social development. In the core of that control is the power of the individual will released through the pathetic outburst caused by the displacement of existential values.

Next the plan for research into the descriptive model of achronia follows four basic steps:

1) measuring the stages of regulated migration in the global socium and the long-term effects on the affected creative communities;

2) Detailed description of the active characteristics of the four types of achronia in view of the positive and negative chronotopes stimulating the mass of individuals in their social actions. Further it is to be connected with the types of cases, the directions of achronia and the changes of environment affecting the formation of global socium.

	Pre-productive age	Productive age
Type 1	+	-
Type 2	+	+
Type 3	-	+
Type 4	-	-

Type 1 includes the social behavior of individuals who have steady positive motivation in their pre-productive age where the self-identification is based on positive social esteem and stimulation of every achievement in the formative years of the growing individual. When the individuals grow out of their training and become of productive age, the stimuli suddenly shift to negative and the creative individuals try to either change the situation or the social environment, or both of them. Thus the individuals of high productive power can become the vehicles of progress helping the rest out of stagnation and crisis. This is the clearest type of achronia that my own generation has gone through during the latest 30 years.

Type 2 occurs when positive stimuli are preserved. The individuals representing this type are rare and can serve as control group allowing to compare and establish the level of displacement of Type 1.

Type 3 is the initially negative case whose parameters shift to positive. This is the group of the keepers of the status of achronia.

Type 4 is entirely negative and can be referred to as 'the lost generation'. A milder negative type is that of the 'haters' who have become popular of late.

3) The third step towards the reconstruction of functioning and complete model of achronia is the measuring of the level of awareness on the part of the governing institutions and individuals of their application of the instruments of achronia. I hypothetically expect that awareness is not necessary as far as logos is obeyed i.e. the application of the rules of good government. Moreover achronia is obscure due to the use of rhetoric in public spaces to describe extreme opposition of control and its avoidance.

Formally there are four possible clear-cut levels of awareness of the use of achronia for social control:

- complete awareness of planned control and strategic targeting of desired effect;
- intuitively followed plan based on sound reason;
- purely intuitive action based on experience and traditionally followed principles of good governing;
- complete unawareness of the capacity of achronia while being guided by the historic processes.

The level of expertise presupposes complete awareness of mechanisms applied and effect planned in detail, yet it does not necessarily imply awareness of the full scope and power of the complex of achronia.

The possibility of applying achronia without being aware of it, suggests the idea that it can be programmed as executive task for an e-government. However, it contains the opposition to such an idea as well: the lack of awareness in a human governor is recompensed for by intuitive decision-taking allowing reasonable risk, sacrifice and error warranted by responsibility and power.

Next we go on to the investigation of the two antinomic sets of techniques that model the two directions of achronia: center bound which is in compliance with the governing strategy, and periphery-bound which models the efforts of the individuals to achieve their freedom of mind and rely on their choice of involvement in social action. Statistics can possibly outline dominant tendencies, but we need a further study of the quality of final effect. In such investigation the rhetorical approach seems to be most suitable to follow.

4) The fourth step next leads to establishing the capacity of achronia as a complex mechanism for acquiring efficiency of an E-government through both adopting and rejecting it in public discourse: the rhetoric features of the social web and the contents of individual stories.[15]

DISCUSSION AND PERSPECTIVES

To sum up, achronia is characterized by four main concepts: 1) awareness, 2) fate /logos; 3) injustice; 4) ethical fundament/value system.

Its further study is outlined as comprising of a number of strategic phases or steps:

1) Planning of social reaction through time in terms of regulation of migration; dislocation and concentration of communities; a Smithsonian approach to current division of labor.

2) Typology of achronia.

3) Varying stages of the awareness of the application of achronia by the governing bodies.

4) Achronia in modelling e-government. Here the study of achronia is based on the rhetoric of the web communities and the antinomies of E-kind.

5) A very recent development involves tracing the dynamic features of achronia in literary texts that establish the ethos of a current culture and support public discourse. A simple model

of off-time migration is achieved, allowing its redirection by means of forming e-culture.

Our thorough approach has been mentalist in nature and its object of interest is social mind.

500 years after the publication of „The Prince" we still need the fundamental theory of Machiavelli as a starting ground for the development of the theory of achronia to serve e-government to the best effect in terms of good reasoning.

In the beginning the idea of achronia looks inseparable from human history and the processes that take place in it. Besides, it has not been included in the theories and mechanisms concerning social governance. However, upon a closer investigation of repeating elements and features of achronia, it arises as a separate social event that is one of the key social clues to e-governing in our time of transcendence of humanity into the virtual worlds created by our changed social minds on the e-platforms of the www. The 'Prince' is no longer bound with the direct exertion of the actions of power and the ethical values of Machiavelli seem to have acquired broader meaning.

I am concerned with this topic because it is closely related with the philosophy of the infosphere in its ethical part where E-kind is seen as a complex global society based on fluctuating communities of real individuals. The problem of power and control are closely connected with the control of information while the actual society has doubled in its social activities. The problem of directed physical migration of creative people seems to have grown larger due to its virtual projection. Therefore, I claim that achronia concerns the social mind in its both ends of functioning as governing and opposition in the structuring of E-kind and extending the existential opportunities of humanity.

It does sound metaphorical. Even today Bulgarian people tend to use two more metaphors to mark its effects: we use the names of *'Absurdistan'* and *'Wonderland'* for marking the geography of the physical frontiers of our being displaced in terms of identifying our belonging to a culture. We cannot move in time physically, that is why we move in space trying to find the Promised land or the value system of our self-respect where the informed and creative individual are the illusory princes of a Self-centered net controlling our lives.

GUESSES INSTEAD OF CONCLUSIONS

Let us accept for a blink of mental unresistance the concept of achronia.

It gives us the freedom of extending an end into a future and discuss it in our presence here and now.

Humankind have no sense of temporality.

They are woven up of universes that are recurring in cyclic redundant modes.

Their recurrence is necessary for intelligent life to map constant coordinates in an incessant process of mutability.

Good and bad are absolute points – the ends of existence and the beginnings of existence. Of which humankind have a sense of survival as logos.

Humanity who have no sense of temporality, cannot have awareness of chronology. Yet, the sense of reasonability rouses the intuition of survival, whether we are aware of it or not. We next weave up ends in the absolute, track routes in eternity, tale tales to be envisioned like stars or black holes.

This makes history vulnerable to circumstances of interpretation that are necessary for the change of intelligent cultures.

Time-machines are controlled through dream-weaving which is not the same as giving or satisfying our wishes.

Its first tool is reading the signs of our existence: those which are engraved in us, and those, which come from the outside. People do not pay attention to what they read. The Language analysis has been underdeveloped for the core of applied linguistics has been slipping away from the attention of philologists. The semantics of a text, not of words is what makes the knowledge of language for the text is the product of language. Thus it is not Applied Linguistic searches but Applied Philology that is the holder of info keys for the latter keeps in view the texture of mentalizing or reality weaving.

Like all human knowledge the language knowledge is not given once and for all but develops and broadens

1. Memory;

2. What is not in language;

3. Connection is of higher analytical level;

4. Visualization;

5. Burnout reserve and the theory of the active fund;

6. Information theory of pain.

Information needs a good flow bringing in and taking out stuff, good connection and clear destination. It needs good browsers and good memory.

The strangest knowledge of the world I received in the evenings of my childhood when my granny and granddad liked to sup in the summer nights in the middle of the front yard below a velvet sky of stars.

Once the stars looked to me like the points of brown-and aubergine tits. Other time they changed the space of illusion and looked like holes.

Granddad pointed at chains of stars and described them to me as figures. Visual illusion could be swallowed down. A child could see the pool of milk spilt on the road and forming the Milky Way or the rose flower covered by shiny drops of diamonds.

But there was the challenge of challenges still ahead.

They are very far away, my granddad said easily. We can see them now as they looked ages ago. Today their form might not look like that at all, neither can we be sure they are still alive. What we see is their light as it started on its route towards us millions of years ago.

I could not take this in. I now wonder how blinded we have been. With all the vast view of Cosmos over our heads, displaying how universe remembers information.

How fascinating it is in fact to know that universe does not forget about you even if you are so small that you can reach to a bit of it millions of years after it has changed.

The memory of the Universe is in its dance where time is excluded.

And next you go to school. And learn math. And learn about time and get inside the blinding fog of fallacy. And forget all about you were been given de fault. How stupid a tiny bit of a mind to imagine it can neglect, shun, decline, debate and doubt the starry night above even if being reminded by philosophers and poets each new age even in unconscious words following unconsciously the texture of universe.

It is not the number, though.

Everything is in language – that builds the poly-dimension language that our minds can read.

The routes do not forget how they got cleaned. The DNA model works independent of time. The DNA model contains immortality. It can only end when it lacks material.

And what is material for dream weaving but star-dust.

End Postulates

- The interconnectedness of all things.
- Theory of redundant models.
- Time is not dimension.
- Achronia is a tool of language.
- Nostalgia is efficient in tales.
- Memory is the key word.
- The memory of universe is motion.
- Digital memory is the remedy for pain.
- G-force and light motion.

BIBLIOGRAPHY AND NOTES

Apostolova, Gergana. 'ACHRONIA AS A COMPLEX MECHANISM FOR SOCIAL CONTROL'. October 2013 in Rhetoric and Communications

No 10: http://rhetoric.bg

Apostolova, G. Persuasive Discourse, Bulgarian, S, 1999

Carnegie, Dale. How to stop worrying and start living, 1948. (Bulgarian translation, S. 1990, Shans Press)

Chomsky, Noam. 'Lectures on Government and Binding' in The Pisa Lectures, 1079-80, MIT Press.

Chomsky, Noam. Media Control, Bulgarian translation, http://chitanka.info/book/2151-mediite_pod_kontrol (last visit 24/03/2014)

Curd, Patricia, A Pre-Socratic Reader: Selected Fragments and Testimonia (Hackett Publishing, 1996), p. 12.

Hofstede, G. Cultures and Organizations: Software of the Mind, 1991, McGraw Hill.

Machiavelli. The Prince. Bulgarian translation in http://chitanka. info/ text/4440-vladeteljat/ (last visit 19/03/2014)

Mavrodieva, Ivanka, Virtual Rhetoric, (Bulgarian). SU Press, 2010

Mavrodieva, Ivanka. RHETORIC and PR, (Bulgarian). SU Press, 2013.

Gofman, A., Moskowitz, H.R., Manchaiah, M., Silcher, M., "Prescriptive Public Policy," Proceedings of IPSI Conference, Montreal, 2006.

Radev, Radi, History of Ancient Philosophy, Sofia, 1981 (in Bulgarian)

Russell, Bertrand, A history of western philosophy. Simon and Schuster, 1945 (reprint) ISBN 0-671-20158-1 Retrieved 2014-03-10 (and the Bulgarian translation).

Dramaliev, Lyubomir. 'Humanism and Moral Crisis' in The Moral Crisis in Our Society – Bulgarian text, Humanity Foundation Press, S, 1994.

Goranov, Krustyo. Moral being of the "'State of Crisis" in The Moral Crisis in Our Society – Bulgarian text, Humanity Foundation Press, S, 1994.

Panev, Baicho. 'Organized Criminality in the Conditions of Economic and Moral Crisis' in The Moral Crisis in Our Society – Bulgarian text, Humanity Foundation Press, S, 1994.

Slanikov, Ivan. 'Crisis and Moral Suffering' in The Moral Crisis in Our Society – Bulgarian text, Humanity Foundation Press, S, 1994.

1   The idea of studying achronia as a fundamental basis for migrations of human productive individuals who have the power of developing the advancement of global culture was first outlined in e-rhetoric in Bulgarian in October 2013 in Rhetoric and Communications No 10: http://rhetoric.bg/: Gergana Apostolova.
'ACHRONIA AS A COMPLEX MECHANISM FOR SOCIAL CONTROL'.

2   Seen in the context of a definition of Hosted as a group of people solving their problems in the same way

3   I have based the choice of the name on the interpretation of its meaning as „out of time", connected with the aesthetics of structuralism: http://facultystaff.ou.edu/L/A-Robert.R.Lauer-1/GenetteDiscours.html Genette, Bachtin, and Tzvetan Todorov; it is also used for denoting the state of the human body in travelling through deep cosmos: Ursula Le Guinn, „The City of Illusions", http:/ /chitanka.info/text/1658/10; a third layer of meaning to be considered is its connecting with fantastic and absurd places and travels in the abstract sense. The event has not happened yet or has already happened: its effect is only marked in the current moment, e.g. „Through the Looking Glass" by L. Carroll, the White Queen's statement: 'Never jam today' (Bulgarian translation by St. Gechev, 1969).

4   Noam Chomsky discusses two aspects of achronia: Plato's problem and Orwell's problem. He also uses the term 'dissident culture'. Media under Control, Bulgarian translation: http://www.savanne.ch/svoboda/anarchy/theory/media.html/; Machiavelli looks into two aspects: the popularity of the Prince and the Fate that needs to be courted: Bulgarian version in http://chitanka.info/text/4440vladeteljat/; aspects of mental displacement are hinted in 'Prince Ferdinand's Advice to his Son' (Bulgarian rare edition); D. Carnegie describes the other side of achronia – the individual exit in his book 'How to control Anxiety'

5   (Bulgarian translation, S. 1990, Shans Press); aspects of achronia are prescriptively laid out in numerous university course books on management and macro economy. I shall not mention here the books of education of the communist government at its state and local institutions and its supporting bodies for social control that formed a network in the system of specific education on all levels of society.

6   E.g. Great Migration, Bulgarian khan Kubrat and his sons; the search for the Promised Land; the settling of America; Crusades; and the great travels round the world.

7   E.g. L. Dramaliev, K. Goranov, B. Panev and I. Slanikov: 'The Moral Crisis in Our Society' – Bulgarian text, Humanity Foundation Press, S, 1994.

8   E.g. The stories of Sindbad from Arabian Nights; Homer's Ulysses, Gilgamesh; Wieland the ironmonger of Valhalla; The tales of Himalayan warriors; the tales of Ural masters from the time of Peter The Great of Russia; the Arthurian legend, etc.

9   American political science, neuroethics; even parodies like Dilbert's Principle and Murphy's Laws. And the Declaration of Independence.[9] Isaak Asimov's series on psychohistory in The Foundation.

10   1Theories mentioned in connection with Lasswell; Gobbels; Poincare; Alfred Ayer, I have previously studied in Apostolova, G. Persuasive Discourse, Bulgarian, S, 1999, and Moscovits et al.

11   Described in all Holy Books and Ancient Histories of Philosophy.

12   Machiavelli, *The Prince*, Op. Cit.

13   On one of Oxford's central squares today there is the grave and the monument to three Oxford professors, burnt for teaching knowledge before its time. In this group the cases of G. Bruno, Galileo, Darwin, and the Bulgarian priest Bogomil, the doctor of Jurisprudence Tzeko Torbov, George Markov etc. also belong.

14   Chomsky's Pisa Lectures

15   Mavrodieva, Ivanka, Virtual Rhetoric, (Bulgarian). SU Press, 2010 and RHETORIC and PR, SU Press, 2013.

The brain, ah, the brain!

What the brain likes to keep:
Not emotions, neither senses
Nor your deeds that you boast of
Just some wishes and some dreams
Sometimes rimes of childish blubber
And strange skills of questioned price;
What remains are just so stories,
Your fears and your games,
How to weave up magic tales,
How to fly and get inside
Each single meme and cell
Singing out mind to life. Probably.